Coming Home

David Guttman

NEWMAN SPRINGS PUBLISHING
320 Broad Street
Red Bank, NJ 07701

First originally published by Newman Springs Publishing 2023

ISBN 979-8-89061-126-0 (Paperback)
ISBN 979-8-89061-127-7 (Digital)

Printed in the United States of America

Based on a true story, except for the parts I could not remember. Those are made up.

Coming home to a place he'd never been before.

—John Denver

To the memory of Dr. Scott Pliskin, DVM

I loved being a doctor, which was odd since I hated almost everything that went along with it. I hated my years of medical school and residency, my nights on call, my beeper, my endless phone calls, my demanding patients, and the practice of medicine in general. I was not a shallow man and had some hatred left over for my ex-wife and her attorney, but most of all, I hated snow. I hated making snowmen, snowball fights, skiing, and anything to do with snow. In the pursuit of my profession, I had endured years in the snow in Omaha, Nebraska and Albany, New York, areas that evidently had never gotten the memo that the Ice Age was over. They said the Eskimos had fifty different words for snow, not including the yellow snow found where the huskies were bedded down for the night, but I had twice that many words to express my hatred for snow. Now I was free of the bonds of my residency and determined to escape to sunshine and warmth.

My plan was to head South and follow the herd of the retired, insured elderly, much like the wolves followed the caribou herd south across the tundra to their winter feeding grounds. I would follow the Cadillacs, Buicks, and RVs south, stopping every few hundred miles at a Sears automotive store, where I would ask about snow tires; when the salesmen had no idea what I was talking about, I would look for a place to practice.

This would be the freshest of fresh starts; I knew nobody that had actually visited, let alone lived in, the South; and with the exception of my training, I had never lived outside New York City. And that didn't really count since it was hard to get a good feel for an area just by looking at it from the windows of the hospital. City lights all looked the same from inside the hospital's windows, and it was hard to distinguish which species of ant you are looking at in the street far below

"This isn't that hard. I've started all over before. I can do this, and it's not as if I have a whole lot to fall back on. Besides, a change will probably be good for me, putting some space between me and my ex, affectionately referred to as the plaintiff, and I never wanted to come to Montgomery to begin with."

Two years earlier, I had just finished *my* residency in pediatrics in Upstate New York and headed south with my wife, our three kids, one dog, and a fifty-thousand-dollar debt. Life was always more exciting than my real life, I did what everyone else did: study the classified ads in specialty medical journals, make phone calls, and attend interviews with promising offers (often the operative word is *promising*, as opposed to *delivering*) in what was cynically noted as the "howdy-shake circuit" To consolidate efforts, we had set up two nearby Alabama practice interviews (one in Phoenix City and one in Montgomery) and followed SOP: meet the doctors, tour the office and hospital, get a quick guided tour of the town and practice, and be all sweetness and smiles, followed by a dress-up dinner where you and your prospective partners could size each other up, which meant analyzing what you drank, what football team you loved, and whether your spouse was too obnoxious or good-looking for the other doctors' wives.

Following unwritten tradition, at the end of the evening, my wife and I said our polite thank-yous and good-nights and retired to our hotel room to dissect every word, glance, and nuance and argue every pro and con of the weekend. By morning we had reached a decision, or actually, we reached two decisions. I chose Phoenix City for its relaxed, small-town flavor; inexpensive housing with enough land to garden and room for the kids to run around; clean air; and lots of places to fish; and my wife chose Montgomery because there was a Casual Corner clothing store at the mall. So we "agreed" to go to Montgomery, which left me the moral high ground if it didn't work out, being able to at least say under my breath, "It was your choice. I told you so."

orty miles of featureless interstate was a good place to have a heart-to-heart, come to Jesus, and talk to yourself; and to the passing motorists, I was probably just singing along with Merle Haggard, Hank, or Elvis… I doubt those passing motorists paid any more attention to me than they did the speed limit, open-container laws, or turn signals. I reminded myself that this was the *New South*, where pickup trucks were being replaced by BMWs with rear-window gun racks and boat hitches. The autopilot interstate trip gave me just enough time to mull over the pros and cons of my decision and do a little self-guided psychotherapy. My thirteen-year marriage was about to end in divorce with a house I would no longer get to live in and three kids I would only be allowed to visit every other weekend, and my office had just announced that because of being "a little short this month," the doctors had decided not to take a salary. Evidently, scheduling conflicts had kept me from knowing about that trivial office meeting, but my partners were very sympathetic, professed to knowing exactly what I was going through, and generally felt my pain. In fact, they had no idea what I was going through. Each of them were calling their portfolio managers to sell some assets and move money into or out of some overflowing stock fund and send a check to fill in for their absent paychecks, while I was probably going to jail for not being able to pay alimony and child support. I doubted they had any idea what I was going through.

Just short of renewing my passport, I heard of a job opening in a little town less than an hour south of Montgomery, and I was once again off on the get a job—howdy-shake circuit. I knew only three things: (1) the town was close enough to my kids that visitation would not be altered, (2) the town needed a pediatrician, and (3) I needed a job. Rumor also had it that I could anticipate getting paid regularly, which would be a welcome change, having decided that as a non-paying hobby, being a doctor left a lot to be desired. If they wanted to talk, I was ready and willing to listen. If I learned nothing else from my defunct marriage, it was to let someone else talk while you just listened.

The trip down to Greenville was certainly pleasant enough, with gently rolling hills through small towns like Letohatchee and Fort Deposit, evidently world-famous as the home of Bates House of Turkey, where tourists heading down to their beach houses in Destin could pick up a ready-cooked reason not to prepare meals for the week. It was also the last "wet" town before entering dry Butler County and a place where the locals loaded up on alcohol and where the law prohibited the sale of alcohol not only to minors and on Sundays but to *everyone* and *always*. If the law also prohibited actually drinking alcohol, it was either the best-kept secret or the most broken law in the state.

Billboards along the roadway advertised boiled peanuts (pronounced bawled), pecan rolls, and tupelo honey as well as bream fingerlings to stock your farm's fishpond. It didn't take me long to figure out I wasn't in Brooklyn anymore, Toto.

I pulled off the interstate at the Greenville exit, made a left onto the main street, and followed the directions I had scribbled down in my hasty phone call a week before. I realized I was running a few minutes late for the appointment, and the slow-moving mud-covered truck I was stuck behind was not going to improve my average speed. The fact that I had no idea what I was actually looking for didn't allow for much speed either; all I knew was that someone named Dr. Paul from the Strickler Clinic was planning to meet me fifteen minutes ago. From behind the smoke-belching truck and just before passing it altogether, I saw two signs, one announcing

Strickler Memorial Hospital and the other announcing Strickler Clinic. The sign listed seven doctors, and most of them were named Strickler. Whoever these people were, there seemed to be a lot of them, and they had all gone into medicine. Great, now I was divorced, unemployed, and outnumbered.

I figured I'd start with the clinic since doctors hated to hang out in hospitals almost as much as patients did. The clinic was a one-story "contemporary" fifties red brick building in the style of Frank Lloyd Wrong and looked like it had been enlarged over the years as needed. I made my way across the fairly full waiting room to the row of glass cubbies staffed by middle-aged female receptionists, each seated beneath a sign with a doctor's name on it. I approached the Dr. Paul Strickler sign and, stooping down, talked through the three-inch hole in the glass. "I have an appointment to see Doctor Strickler" at two o'clock," I said, hoping she would avoid reminding me it was now two fourteen.

"Well, which Doctor Strickler, hon?" she asked pleasantly. "Dr. Paul, Vernon Sr., Vernon Jr., or Dr. Aubrey?"

Although I was standing in front of her line and she was sitting under the Dr. Paul sign, I avoided the temptation to point out the obvious, recalling that I was unemployed and definitely outnumbered as well as that they had the home-field advantage.

"I guess I should have clarified that my appointment is with Dr. Paul," I offered.

She handed me a clipboard with New Patient Visit written on the top and asked me to bring it back to her as soon as I completed my health history, insurance information, and demographics. I explained that I was not a new patient, and I guessed that it was then she noticed I was the only one in the waiting room in a coat and tie. "If you are a pharmaceutical representative, hon, you can give me your card, and I'll see if one of our doctors can see you for a few minutes. But usually, we see you folks only first thing in the morning." Leaning closer to the little glass porthole, she stage-whispered, "And it helps a lot if you bring donuts, especially the strawberry-filled kind, though I'm partial to Hardee's biscuits myself."

It seemed I was not going to get by this lady without a bit more candor and a lot more Southern charm. I noticed her nameplate said Nell, so the next time I spoke into our little hole in the glass, I said, "Ms. Nell, ma'am, I sure would appreciate it if you could tell Dr. Paul Strickler that Dr. Guttman, the pediatrician from Montgomery he spoke to, is here and would like to see him."

With that, the sky opened up, light came down from the heavens, Nell's face split in two with a smile, and she gushed, "Well, hon, why didn't you say so? You come on right back" as she took me by the arm and escorted me through the reception area, proudly showing me off to the clinic staff like some prized sport trophy fish she had just landed. "This is Doctor Guttman, the pediatrician who came down from Montgomery to see us and maybe help us out."

I felt like I was being led down a long windowless tunnel with doors on either side, some of which were adorned with names of this doctor or that to guide me on my way, though not especially helpful in my case since it seemed most of the doctors had the same last name. Two even had the same first name. The staff that lined the hallway formed an ad hoc receiving line and through smiling lips murmured, "We've all been waiting to meet you, hon. We're so excited to be getting a new pediatrician. The children have been without a doctor for almost a year, and our other doctors, well… They're good doctors and all, but they need to stick to grown-up folks. Did you say you were from Montgomery? Are your people from Alabama? Which school did you go to, hon, Alabama or Auburn? We sure hope you'll like it here. This is a real fine town to raise your family. Can I get you a Co Cola? Sweet tea? Coffee?"

I nodded politely, and since it was evident the questions were not really intended to draw answers, and treated my newfound admirers to the best-polished howdy shake I knew how to do. I figured this was probably not the best time to confess I was really born and raised in New York and had actually gotten educated outside of Alabama.

At last, Nell opened the door labeled Dr. Paul Strickler and deposited me into a small office just big enough for an oak desk and an executive chair facing the entrance, two guest chairs, and one window on the rear wall, framed by an overflowing bookcase on either side and a large collection of statues of frogs, which I later learned was Paul's passion.

"Dr. Paul will be out in just a minute, hon," Nell said, leaving me to wonder if I could at least get her to address me as "Dr. Hon."

Left to myself, I took in my surroundings. There was the compulsory ego wall to one side, covered with certificates and diplomas attesting that the doctor you were about to entrust your health with was duly educated, licensed, and certified. I had often wondered if patients wouldn't be better served if physicians displayed their transcripts rather than their diplomas so you could tell if the doctor you were about to entrust your life and limb with did well in the medical field relating to your particular problem (e.g., "Gee, Doc, you got an A in cardiology but almost flunked orthopedics, and I have this sprained ankle"). I sometimes thought we were probably best not knowing certain of the finer points of our doctor's education. Opening into either side of the room was a numbered exam room door, each with a plastic chart holder. I made a mental note that one plastic holder held a medical chart and that other was empty; and since I could make out a man's voice coming from behind the door with the empty holder, I concluded that Dr. Paul was indeed behind door number one (just like on the quiz show). So far so good, and at least there was no stuffed deer head or largemouth bass mounted on walls.

While I was humming the tune to "Deliverance" to myself, door number one opened, and Dr. Paul entered the room, or more correctly, he completely filled the doorway, eclipsed the room, and filled all the available space not already occupied by me and the furniture. He was enormous both in height and width, wearing an open short-sleeve white shirt that had long ago given up the battle to stay tucked in trousers that fit only by being positioned well below what would have been his waistline.

He stuck out a massive hand. "Paul Strickler, and you must be David Guttman, the baby doctor from New York," he said as a smile filled his face, which at least started to decrease my terror. "Have a seat, son. You must be tired from that trip all the way down from Montgomery. Can I offer you any-thing to drink, or more correctly, offer you any-thing these damn county officials will allow us to drink since they voted liquor out? You see, I know every damn one of those self-righteous hypocritical fools on the county commission, and to a man, they are the biggest bunch of drunks in the county. Anyway, they seem to have stopped short of searching our houses for alcohol, where we take every opportunity to make up for what's not permitted in public. Before we went dry, there was even an enterprising young fella who made a replica of the gun-smoke bar The Longbranch, complete with a hitching post and a sign overhead that read 'Long Branch Saloon.' Those self-righteous city councilmen evidently didn't appreciate the marketing value and objected to the word *saloon*, dredging up some old statutes restricting the advertising of liquor and forcing him to remove the word *saloon* from that sign, just not to be undone, and replace it with one that said 'Long Branch Whore House.' I guess they concluded the original sign wasn't so bad after all and let the designation *saloon* remain."

"First of all, Dr. Strickler," I started—before he cut me off, saying, "The doctor title was just for patients, pharmacy reps, and the Rotary Club. We all call one another by our Christian names, and the staff just adds *Dr.* in front of that. So I'm Paul to you, Dr. Paul to my nurse, and Dr. Strickler to my *vast* flock of patients I call the worried well."

I decided it was not a good idea to ask him if Jewish people had Christian names, recalling the wrath of my orthopedics professor when I asked him if Muslims and Jews actually had hamstrings. "Well, Paul, I want to apologize for being late. I got stuck behind a truck that decided to tour the town in first gear."

He laughed and corrected me that this was a really small town and that I had gotten behind *the* truck, and around here, anything within one hour was considered inordinately punctual.

"There are several ways we can handle this, but what I suggest is that I give you the canned discourse on the clinic, hospital, and town, accidently forgetting to mention all the bad points, and then you can tell me all the *good* points about yourself, omitting anything you never told your mama. Then, when we are done lying to each other, we can tour the place and meet the other doctors. Does that sound okay to you?"

"Sounds fine to me," I said, then added, "and by all means, you go first. Sounds like you have a lot more ground to cover."

He leaned back in his chair, crossed his arms behind his head, and began. "This clinic was started by my grandfather, a general practitioner originally from Scotland with a bit of Ireland thrown in. He had six children, two of whom were foolish enough to go into medicine, my uncle Aubrey, who retired a few years ago from urology, and my daddy, who is a general surgeon, and his office is right down the hallway from me. He's seventy-eight years old, sharp as a tack, makes rounds every day, operates whenever we let him, and shows absolutely no sign of slowing down. He did his surgical training at Harvard, has never come to work without a tie and jacket, and delivered most of the people who live in this county. I don't think you will ever hear him raise his voice at work to get anyone in line.

Mama took care of that at home, and I take care of that here.

"Anyway my uncle Aubrey, we now call Dr. Aubrey senior since he has a son, Aubrey junior, who specializes in otolaryngology and practices in the new wing we added on a few years ago. He is superbly trained, hardworking, and by far the best-looking Strickler to come out of this family. I think half his female patients deliberately roll in pollen just to have an excuse to see him. If you want to see what disappointment looks like, watch them the first time they see his wedding ring or, better yet, when they get a look at his wife, a former Miss University of Alabama.

"Anyway, Aubrey is a whole lot better-looking than the rest of the Strickler clan, and I like to remind him, therefore, who got the brains in the family.

My daddy's side produced two doctors, me and my brother, Vernon Jr. I'm an internist, which around here means I treat everyone but kids, deliver babies when I absolutely have to, and do some suturing and emergency procedures but nothing my surgeon brother or father would ever mistake for surgery. My brother, Vernon, did his surgical residency in New York City's Roosevelt Hospital and then was a MASH surgeon in Vietnam for two years. He came home with all his parts and, more importantly, a surgical assistant, Nurse Robert Crenshaw, who is an absolute wiz at suturing, casting, orthopedics, and just about anything my illustrious brother wants him to do.

"So at the present time, there are four Stricklers in the clinic along with two other docs, Ed

McCallaster, who started out life as an Annapolis cadet, and Danny Godwin, a local boy from just down the road from here, an even smaller town called Georgiana, where he was the star of his high school football team and then graduated from pharmacy school before seeing the light and becoming a doctor.

"So our clinic consists of two surgeons, three internists, one ear-nose-and-throat man, and, as of six months ago, no pediatrician. Not to overstate the obvious, we need to hire one, but we're not looking for just anyone. We all have roots in this community, some going back three generations. These are not just our patients. These are our neighbors, the people we went to elementary school with, and their parents, aunts, and uncles. We not only care for these people, but we also care about them. And I mean all these folks, young, old, rich, and poor, and in case you are wondering, Blacks and Whites. We never turn away anyone. We never have or will use a collection agency, expecting people pay us what they can when they can. And we all live comfortably. Occasionally, we get paid through services like mowing our lawns or washing our cars, but these patients pay us when and how they can. I never want to hear that someone went without groceries or books for their kids to pay my bill.

"If you decide to join us, we expect you will adopt the same attitude. It's a two-way street. You show these folks you care about them, and they'll do the same to you. We do not want to get rich over someone else's poor health or misfortune. Don't get me wrong, we like to get rich, but we do it through the investments we make with the money we earn from medicine, not from medicine itself."

I found myself trying to wrap my mind around what I had just heard. These were not a bunch of backwoods country doctors scraped together from the bottom of the medical barrel. They had trained at Harvard and New York City and were board-certified internists or surgeons. One had a an additional degree in pharmacy, and one had been a MASH surgeon in Vietnam.

With CVs like that, they could have their pick of practice opportunities, but they were here in Greenville. And from what I had gathered, they were not here for the money but to practice medicine the way I thought it should be. I made a mental note that when it came my tum to discuss my side of the getting-to-know-each-other that I *be a* little less impressed with myself.

"My granddaddy L. V. Strickler graduated from the Vanderbilt med school in 1898, and he eventually moved to Greenville and went into practice with his brother, Andrew Lee Strickler, in 1916, opening the first Strickler infirmary.

"That burned to the ground in 1921, and Dr. L. V. built a new facility consisting of a dozen patient rooms, a kitchen, a lab, and of all things, an X-ray just like the big boys had. We added onto the building every few years. A general surgeon, Vernon, joined the practice in 1932, and his baby brother, Aubrey, a urologist, came aboard in 1940. Since then, every generation of the Stricklers has seen fit to produce more doctors to keep the place going. Now, understand that in our family, there is never any pressure when it comes to career choice. We are free to go to any medical school we choose, assuming we can get accepted.

"Today the clinic building shares a parking lot with the hospital itself and is a separate corporate entity, except that they are both named Strickler and that the family foundation owns them both. The hospital is approved for forty-five beds, and we run about 75 percent full, although during flu season, any flat surface we can fit a mattress on top of and hang an IV from might become a bed.

"We actually have an emergency room, and we call it that. It's not an emergency department. It's one room, one nurse, and one doctor on call. Speaking of which, we all take the ER call, and that usually scares the pants off pediatricians, especially when dealing with heart attacks, strokes, and gunshot wounds. What we expect is that somewhere during four years of medical school, the professors beat enough general information into our skulls that we can do some assessment and triage and hold things together until the cavalry arrives. If it's any consolation, we're all terrified when it comes to taking care of infants and little kids. Call is one out of seven right now. There is a solo family doctor in town on our call schedule and one out of eight if you join us. There is some complex calendar we make up six months at a time. That basically leaves you on call one out of seven weekends, which I think is pretty damn livable. Any questions so far? You look a little green."

"Well, actually, I am what you might call a little rusty on general medicine, surgery, obstetrics, urology, cardiology, and neurosurgery and not sure I feel comfortable about anything other than pediatrics at this time. Would I have to deliver babies?"

"Hell, nobody says you have to feel comfortable. All we ask is that you do it. It's the patient we're trying to make comfortable, and seriously, we expect there will be a break-in learning period we'll help you adjust to. And what does not come back to you or was never there to begin with, we will teach you. As far as delivering *babies, we* don't do any planned obstetrics, but some folks refuse to get the message and, despite nine months to make other arrangements, wait at home until they know the contractions are too close together for us to send them up to Montgomery, not really giving us a choice. On the bright side, the nurse will usually have that baby wrapped in a blanket and taking his first bottle by the time you drive in from home, and we make a point of not living too damn close to the hospital." He added a wink. "Feeling better now?"

While I tried breathing exercises and thinking about my happy place to bring my newly generated anxiety under control, Paul glanced at his watch while he dialed the phone. "If you don't have any pressing need to get back on the road, we'd be pleased if you could join me and my bride for some authentic Southern cooking."

I wasn't sure it was a question, but to be on the safe side, I said, "Sure," but I didn't think he was really waiting for an answer.

"Hey, Mama, we should be finished up here in an hour or so, and the good doctor has agreed to eat with us poor country folks this evening. We got any leftovers we can pass off as authentic Southern cooking?… Just about anything will do. I believe he's from New York, so anything we feed him will be better than what he's used to… Okay, we'll be home after a while." He looked up at me, patted his belly, and said, "I'm just messing with you. Do I look like the sort of person who has leftover food around the house?"

I asked him how long he had been married since he referred to his wife as his bride.

He smiled and said, "We've been married for thirty-seven years, but I'll always think of her and treat her as my bride. Let's go for a quick tour of the clinic, and then we can say hi to the other doctors. They should be wrapping up around four thirty, and we'll meet in the library."

*****

The rest of the clinic looked pretty much like the part I had already seen on the way to Paul's office—not too bad but could definitely benefit from some fresh paint.

"There's always been an unwritten law that doctors have to take some time off during the week, I guess to play golf or something, but we try to stagger it so we have no less than four docs here at a time. And that includes at least one surgeon and one internal medicine doc. Since there's only room for one pediatrician, you'll have to be here all the time," Paul said without a smile, but by now I picked up that he was messing with me again.

"That sounds fair. Wouldn't want it any other way." I messed with him.

We peeked into a few of the exam rooms along the hallway, each containing the customary exam table, a doctor roll-around stool, and a small writing desk with the usual collection of examination instruments like glass jars of cotton swabs and tongue blades (or what pediatricians call choke-'em sticks). While not fancy, they were neat, clean, and well lit with natural light from one window in each room.

Entering the business wing, we were greeted by the office manager, Ms. Velma Higgins.

"Dr. Guttman, I want you to meet our office manager, Ms. Velma Higgins," Paul said as he led me over to a fortyish woman who looked a lot like every social studies teacher I ever had. "She runs the place, keeps us all in line, and makes sure the patients are all happy, even if that means occasionally we are not."

She smiled, shook my hand, and said, "I know you just like to tell everyone that story, Dr. Paul, but it's just not true. The last time I checked, you, your brother, and your daddy had the last word around here. I'm so glad you're interested in joining our little group, and I hope you like what you've been shown so far. If there is anything I can do to help you, please don't you hesitate to ask." She nodded her head and returned to her desk, indicating she was too busy to chat anymore.

When out of earshot, Paul said, "Velma started working for us when she was seventeen. She sat in a corner of the operating room while my daddy performed surgery and dictated surgical reports and progress notes about some other cases. We didn't have dictating equipment back then, and Daddy didn't have time to do it after surgery. He and his brother would usually get home from the hospital around 9:00 PM, and by 7:00 AM the next day, Velma had left all his completed dictations typed on his desk for signature. She has no formal education beyond high school, but over the years, she has taken over running the day-to-day business of this clinic. And that can involve riding herd on six rather large egos. Sure, we get the last word around here. As long as it's 'Yes, ma'am.'"

After the business-office tour, we entered the new wing added when Dr. Aubrey, the ear-nose-and-throat doctor, came back home from residency. It was like a trip through a time machine. Here the lighting was intense, and the exam and procedure rooms tastefully appointed and state-of-the-art, with a full X-ray suite, a complete laboratory, a cast room, and an outpatient minor surgical room.

Paul waved his arm around to take this all in. "This is what we had to put up to get my little cousin to come back from Birmingham. He better stay here long enough to get it paid for. Let's wander down to the conference room so you can meet the rest of the doctors, size one another up, and so forth," he said as I vainly tried to keep up with his stride as he led me down the hallway. From halfway down the hallway, I could tell that we were not the first to arrive and that there was already a heated discussion going on among the other doctors.

"Looks to me like Bear has no choice but to go with the shotgun against Tennessee," came a voice from the conference room. "Their defense has been just murdering everyone, and frankly, with the lack of depth Bama has at quarterback this season, we just can't risk an injury to our star passer.

"That kid has a hell of an arm, but if he doesn't learn to scramble out of the pocket when he sees a wall of orange jerseys coming at him, they're gonna carry him off the field. Like most of 'em, they've learned to be more afraid of Coach Bryant in the locker room than the opposition on the field."

"Another voice added in, "It doesn't help that coaches of half the SEC teams we face today were assistant coaches or players under Coach Bryant at one time or another. They may not be able to read his mind, but they sure as hell can remember his playbook."

"Well, maybe if he varied it from time to time, that would confuse them into thinking the Bear actually came up with some new plays. Doesn't he have enough improvising to do just to cover injuries and arrested players? Last week we had so many Bama linemen locked up in the Tuscaloosa jail that they were thinking of changing the team motto from 'Roll Tide' to 'Parole Tide.'"

As we rounded the corner and entered, I was able to merge the voices in the hallway together with four men standing at one end of the room.

Obviously the oldest, a tall man in a suit and tie and with a full head of slightly graying hair combed straight back with some streaks of white extended his hand. "I'm Dr. Vernon Sr. We're pleased to have you in our little town. I hope Paul has had a chance to tell you a little about us."

"Yes, Pop, I've told him *everything* but where we hid the skeletons from the previous applicants," Paul replied as he took two Cokes from the table and handed me one, which I took to mean, "Drink this. You're gonna need it."

Dr. Vernon took my hand, literally and figuratively. Not only was his hand much bigger than mine, but also, he gave no indication he planned to let go anytime soon. I had offered my hand in greeting, but evidently, around here that was something like giving your hand in marriage.

Still holding my hand, Dr. Vernon turned me to meet the other doctors and didn't so much as release my hand as pass it onto the next person to shake and to hold until he tired of it too and was willing to pass it on.

In quick succession, I met Dr. Vernon Jr., a sandy-haired, soft-spoken, smaller version of Paul's dad, and Aubrey, the movie-star, eye-candy doctor I had been briefed on; and I was about to shake hands with Dr. Danny Hall, a cherubic sort of man with an ingrained smile and self-effacing manner, when Paul pulled my hand away, saying, "He's the one who went to Auburn. It's best not to physically touch him any more than you have to. Never know if it's contagious."

Danny just smiled and took my hand anyway, signaling that since neither of us attended Alabama, we would team up to share the ridicule and soon be friends.

"Let's all have a seat and get acquainted," Vernon said as he eased down into the seat at the head of the table and waved the rest of us into the seats on either side. Paul took the seat directly to his father's right; I was seated across from him, to Vernon's left; and the others seated themselves in a way that made me realize there was definitely an understanding, if not an absolute rule, about who was who in this clinic and where they were expected to fit in—the same way a herd of horses will file into their assigned stalls when brought into the bam at night to feed. Dr. Vernon Sr. was definitely in charge, and Paul was literally and figuratively his right-hand man.

"Well, Dr. Guttman, or may I call you Dr. David? As I said, we're all pleased that you are interested in joining our little clinic and helping us out here in Greenville. One of our doctors, Ed McCallaster, is off today, either playing golf or flying that foolish airplane of his around. And while we had hoped for enough rain to force him to change his plans for both and join us, it looks like the weather didn't cooperate, and you'll have to put off that pleasure for later. I've told him that the two things insurance companies around here hate to underwrite is a colored man with a chain saw or a doctor with an airplane, but he's too hardheaded to listen.

"Anyway, we've had a chance to read through your résumé, and l must say it was really impressive. But if you wouldn't mind spending a few minutes and telling us about yourself and how you came to be interested in Greenville and us.?"

I realized now why Paul had given me the Coke as I walked in. I wished this interview wasn't happening in a dry county.

Recalling that my divorce had given me considerable experience with ad-lib testifying, l decided on the short, canned version. I told Dr. Vernon he could call me anything but Dave since my mother hated that name. Speaking of my mother, when I graduated from medical school, my mother said that she could now call me a doctor. I said, "Thanks, Mom. Now I know what the PhD I've had for six years meant to you."

"I'm 37 years old, recently divorced after 13 years, have 3 children, two boys, 9 and 7, one daughter, age 2. I went to undergraduate school upstate New York, at St. Lawrence University, graduated in '64, and got my M.D. from Creighton University in Omaha, in 1975, followed by a residency in Pediatrics in Albany New York Medical Center from 1975 till 1978. After college and before med school I went to graduate school and got a master's degree in medical entomology from Cornell University in 1966 and a Ph.D. in parasitology from Tulane University in New Orleans 1970, and spent several years in Colombia, doing research in entomology and parasitology, pretty much chasing bugs through the Colombian rainforest. For the last three years I have been employed in Montgomery as a general pediatrician in a four-doctor pediatric group and on the staff of Baptist and St. Margaret's hospitals."

"Now, did I hear you right?" Aubrey interrupted, half laughing. "Did you say you got a PhD in parapsychology? Isn't that the study of the paranormal, clairvoyance, telepathy, and the like?"

"Yes, it is, Aubrey, and I therefore knew you were going to ask that question." I decided that if Aubrey wanted to match wits and be cute, I would be cuter. He might be the coolest thing Greenville had ever seen, but I was from New York, and we Yankees had a reputation of being smart-ass wise guys to uphold.

"Actually, the PhD was in parasitology, the study of parasites."

Backpedaling a bit, he countered with "Well, what does a parasitologist do in Montgomery, Alabama?" still holding his face in a glued-on smile.

I guessed that not wanting to be outdone by this Yankee in their midst or relishing the chance to take his cousin down a notch himself, Paul chimed in. "Hell, Aubrey, it's the seat of government of the great state of Alabama. Where else would you look for parasites around here?"

I cast a grateful glance over at Paul while we enjoyed the laughter of all but Aubrey.

"I was born in Brooklyn, New York, home of the world-famous Brooklyn Dodgers, who I assume you've heard of, and lived there until I left for college at age seventeen. Outside of medicine, until recently, I spent my time tending to the needs of my kids and the wants of my wife, which were not necessarily compatible, nor did I do those things in that order. Now I pretty much have refocused *on the* kids, lawyers, and getting my life back together with perhaps a little time for gardening, fishing, and bluegrass music. Since I'm unsure of what else you want to know, maybe I could just answer any questions you have." I hoped they would be just as eager to get out of this suddenly small and rapidly shrinking room, and Paul and I could beat a hasty retreat.

"I'm curious. You said you grew up in New York City," Vernon Jr. interjected, "and I'm sure you noticed coming down here from Montgomery that Greenville is a small town and that there isn't a lot to it. I love the place because I was born here, as was almost all my family unless their folks were out of town when it came time to come into the world, and then they got back here as soon as circumstances would let them. I guess you heard that I did my surgical residency in New York and spent a few years in Vietnam, but there was never any doubt that as soon as the army was done with me, I headed home to Greenville to work alongside my daddy. Have you ever lived in a small town? How do you think you'll make the adjustment?"

I began to realize that I was in uncharted waters, trying to take an exam that I forgot to study for, but if med-school rounds taught me one thing, it was how to sound like you knew what you were talking about despite almost overwhelming ignorance: answer the professors' questions at least as well as your classmates and, as soon possible, escape from the hot seat and look up the right answer for next time.

"To begin with, I said was that I was born in Brooklyn, which is part of New York City in a way, but in a way, it is not New York City, as you may be picturing in your minds. I grew up in a neighborhood, not the whole city. I lived in the same apartment house my parents brought me home from the hospital to when I was born until I left for college. We lived in one neighborhood, defined by which high school we went to *or* would go to when we got old enough, and I only rarely went outside our unwritten boundaries. There were certain playgrounds, candy stores, and movies in our neighborhood, and that was where we stayed. I don't mean to say we never left our turf, but when we took the bus or subway to another area to go to a show, Coney Island, the beach, or a museum, it was a really big deal. When we actually ventured into Manhattan, we said we were 'going into the city,' and there were certain areas of New York where we never would go to.

"My apartment house, which was home to about fifty families, was really *my* small town. I was friends with the same kids who lived in the building the whole time I lived there. After school we'd be in one another's apartments, and at dinnertime, my mom would just call around on the house phone to see where I had ended up and tell me my dad was home from work and to come home. So in some ways, I lived in a 'town,' but mine was vertical and a lot smaller than Greenville. And we also did so to be near family. My father was one of ten children, and my mother, one of six. Most of my relatives lived right around us, and to make it a little more confusing and cut down on the numbers, my father and two of his brothers married my mother and two of her sisters. So we had three brothers married to three sisters and a whole bunch of double cousins.

"My grandma lived a half block away. She was my favorite person in my world, and when I ran away from home, usually about once a week, with just my comic books and underwear, my mom knew exactly where to look for me. She'd call Grandma and 'ask' her to send me home before ruining my dinner with her famous chocolate chip cookies. Grandma had her 'secret' cookie recipe, which we later found out she got from the box of Toll House morsels.

"There were aunts and uncles nearby, and most of our social life was either with them, neighbors in the building, or friends my parents had since they were themselves kids. And did I mention that I hated living in New York and would rather be a greeter at Walmart than a doctor in New York City? My high school graduation class was 1,300 students, and we took up the biggest theater in Brooklyn for two days. After four years, I think I knew twenty people including those from my building.

"The only thing that saved me from Brooklyn was that my family would leave Brooklyn every summer and head up to the Catskills, to a resort just outside of Ellenville, New York, and it was there that I flourished. The hotel and surrounding cabins could hold about one hundred guests, and we pretty much went to the same place from the time I was an infant until high school when I became old enough to work there. This place was set in the woods except for some pasture to play softball, and I planned my whole winter around what I would do the next summer. As soon as we unpacked, I would grab my BB gun, which was locked up all winter, and head out into the woods to spend the day messing around in the creeks and forests. Each year, my friends and I would build a lean-to shack as soon as we could escape from our parents, and we'd roast hot dogs and marshmallows every few evenings.

"By the time I was ready for college, I realized that I needed to be in a smaller group away from the city and picked a small liberal arts college that was only 2,500 students in all four years, and that was just big enough for me. I had learned that I was really a small-town kid stuck in a big city. And for what it's worth, I never wanted to go to Montgomery to begin with. I preferred a small town on the Georgia-Alabama state line. It was my wife who picked Montgomery." I looked around the room. They were not falling asleep after my monologue, nor were they laughing.

Vernon shook his head a little and said, "Well, you know I did my surgical training at Roosevelt Hospital in 'the city,' as you call it, and more than once thought about building a campfire in Central

Park and cooking weenies, but figured I'd get mugged or arrested, or both."

"You indicated you like to fish. What kind of fishing do you do?" Danny asked.

"I like all kinds of fishing except I've not had much experience with fly-fishing, which looks like a lot of work and a good chance at drowning. Most of the time, it seems what fly fishermen catch is about the size of bait used for other kinds of fishing. I pretty much claim that I'm fishing for whatever I catch and take credit for it.

"Whatever I come home with, that's what I say I was out fishing for. I depend pretty heavily on structure when I fish, and the structure I most rely on is the other fishermen. I assume these local fishermen in the other boats know way more about what they are doing than some transplanted Yankee."

Mercifully, I heard Dr. Vernon clear his throat, signaling that it was time for everyone else to relinquish the microphone. "David, we've had a nice visit and got a chance to get acquainted, and before Paul steals you away and stuffs you full of Southern hospitality, I have one last question. I have to warn you this maybe a deal-breaker, so think really hard and take your time before you answer."

I could sense a palpable tension come over the room and thought that even the air conditioner was making less noise.

Dr. Vernon continued, "Are you an Alabama football fan or an Auburn fan? We already have one of those heretics in our midst, and I am afraid another traitor to the Crimson Tide might upset the natural order of things around here or at least give my colleague Danny the impression of acceptability."

I had decided a while ago that this place was a combination of *Marcus Welby, MD,* and *Father Knows Best*, and if I wanted to get accepted into this pack, I better please the alpha male and work on the rest of the alphabet later. "We'll, sir, I'm actually a little surprised you asked that question. I didn't realize there was another football team around here."

"You got that exactly right." Dr. Vernon chuckled. "There are indeed other teams, even what some might call football teams, but they don't amount to much when they face Bear Bryant and the Crimson Tide. Seems like you got the right answer" he said as he nodded at Paul.

Everyone shook my hand as they headed out the door except for Danny, who leaned close and said, "When we get a chance, let me tell you about Auburn. I hope you like what you saw and heard so far and will be back. Welcome aboard."

Paul said, "Give me a few minutes to close things up in my office, and then we'll run over to the house before my wife starts putting my picture on milk cartons and packing up my clothes for Goodwill. I'll meet you outside the front door. If that Coke I fed you has worn out its welcome, the bathroom is down the hall, third door on left. Yes, we do have indoor plumbing, and no, we don't have a pile of corncobs in there."

Left alone for the first time in about four hours, I tried unsuccessfully to organize what I had seen, weigh the pros and cons, and prioritize them. I realized that would have to wait till I was alone, and while there wouldn't be arguments now that I was divorced, there wouldn't be anybody to help me sort things out either. There was now only one opinion, one voice in what I was to do, and no one to blame later on for the wrong decision. I could screw up my life as much as I wanted.

I found an unlocked door and let myself out, noticing that the clinic and adjoining hospital, while taking up most of the block, were situated on a tree-lined residential street lined with well-maintained houses with wide porches that had Norman Rockwell–ish rocking chairs. If it were not for the noise from the air conditioners,

I bet I could have actually heard birds singing. There were a few people out on the street, and almost without exception, they all said hi or nodded to me as they passed. Had Paul and Velma told everyone in Greenville that I was coming, or were these the curious who wanted to see an actual New York doctor for themselves? I found myself nodding back and was occasionally asked how I was doing.

Paul came up behind me. "Why don't you leave your car here? I'll drop you back after supper, assuming you'll be sober enough to drive, and that way, you won't get lost trying to follow me to the house or stuck behind *the* truck again and miss supper altogether. Along the way, I can show you a little bit of the town. Contrary to what Papa thinks, there's more to this place than the clinic and the hospital."

*****

He led me in the general direction of a parking shed along one wall of the now-empty clinic parking lot, unlocked a large late-model Buick sedan, and squeezed himself behind the wheel while I got in the other side. As I was fumbling to retrieve a half-buried seat belt, we began to pull out onto the street, and it was only after a few more minutes in my automotive archeological dig that I managed to untangle what was obviously a rarely used seat belt. I thought for a moment of reminding Paul about his belt but didn't want to ask in case his reason for not using one was that they just didn't fit around him.

Paul must have seen me glance over at him and had obviously gotten some training in parapsychology himself. "I know you were going to remind me about my seat belt, but you resisted the urge to give me the canned Rotary Club 'Seat Belts Save Lives' lecture. And since Yankees are not known for their tact, I'm curious why you didn't say anything. For what it's worth, I usually wear the damn thing when I drive out of town even if I've had to install a belt extension."

"Well, now you're making it too easy, Paul. Do you want to hear the canned lecture I give to schools and civic groups about seat belts saving lives and the fact that a great majority of accidents occur within five miles of home?"

"No, not if you can possibly control yourself. I don't want to hear it. I've heard it all before, and I'm sure as hell not stupid enough to dredge out some story about some Bubba I heard of over the next county who swears he would have been killed if he *had* been buckled in and only lived to tell about it because he wasn't wearing a seat belt. I know the stats, same as you.

"Here's the thing. This is a small town. We got seven doctors, but only two are surgeons, my kid brother Vernon and my father. They handle all the trauma, all the car wrecks. There's no one else. If I'm in a bad crash, I don't want to make it to the hospital and have one of them not be able to save me and lose me on their operating table.

"I love them dearly, and there's really nothing I wouldn't do for either of them. Literally, I mean it.

I would rather die than lay that burden on them. When I'm away from Greenville, sure, I want those doctors to do whatever it takes to help me survive as long as some other surgeon has to live with my death, not my daddy or kid brother."

"I have to admit that makes a lot of sense, and it's not at all what I expected to hear. But it's still more than a little crazy," I answered. "I assume since your dad and brother just met me, they'll be okay if I die, so I can wear my belt?" I asked.

"Sure, no one's going to get too worked up over one less Yankee. It's not like you all are in short supply these days. I guess you've heard the one about Northerners being like hemorrhoids. Once they come down, they never go back up, and they're a pain in the ass the whole time they're here." He looked over to me and added, "Hope I didn't offend you."

"No, not at all, but for a group that likes to take pride in their hospitality and graciousness, you Southerners sure are a bunch of sore losers. And it's not like we started the war," I added with a laugh.

Sensing it was probably time to change the subject rather than stage a Civil War reenactment in the front seat of his car right here and now, Paul turned onto Commerce Street, obviously the main business area of the town. "The town was built around this street, anchored at one end by the railroad station and the other by the courthouse. The courthouse is in the middle of a traffic circle now, but when it was put up, it was the end of town. Since Greenville's the county seat, the town and the county both do their business from the same building. The municipal court's on the ground floor, along with the probate office and the clerk's office to pay traffic tickets, register births and deaths, and so forth. Upstairs is where the county rules. It's pretty much a repetition of what you see downstairs except you have to walk up a flight of stairs to get there. They do seem to handle more important trials, and the lawyers adjust their fees accordingly. The courthouse circle itself is fringed with a wreath of attorneys' offices, bail-bond offices, accounting firms, and the lunch shops that fuel everything, and it's where the real business of the law is conducted."

"Is the police station down there too?" I asked.

"No, come to think of it, they are closer to the other end of town. I guess they didn't want their day-to-day activities to be unduly influenced by the law," Paul answered with a chuckle.

Along both sides of the street were rows of small shops and storefronts covered with awnings and set back on curbs that were raised at least a few steps above the street level. Most appeared to be in reasonably good condition, and there were only occasional empty ones.

"At one time, all the commerce was conducted on this one street, hence the name Commerce Street. Farmers and their families would come into town on Saturdays and purchase what they needed for the week, but mainly they socialized, the men at the hardware store, the women at the dry goods and clothier's, and the kids, of course, at the soda shop. The storefronts were *always* shielded from the sun and rain by those metal awnings hung out front, and since we didn't have sewers, the curbs were raised up to avoid flooding.

"The South is famous for its rain, and when it rains here, it rains hard and long. You know, that's where we get the expression 'raining cats and dogs.' When it rains so hard, the animals wash down the street. Around here that's called a gully washer. Anyway, the stores stayed open on Saturdays, and then they closed on Wednesday afternoons. Still do, even the post office, though I have no damn idea how the federal employees get away with sneaking that day off past Washington.

"Now that we have the interstate cutting through town, some of the shops are moving out that way, and you can't walk to and from all the stores in town anymore. Nor are they shielded with awnings. Someday we'll probably put up some kind of fancy mall out there to be really modern and once again be able stay dry while walking to do our shopping, real modern, just like one hundred years ago." As we swung around the courthouse and continued back up the street, Paul asked, "Do you know what two structures every town in the South has to have, not counting a Baptist church on every corner? There has to be a courthouse square, and somewhere there has to be a statue of a Confederate soldier. That soldier is always facing north to defend against the Union Army."

As if on cue, a small park appeared on our left with a life-size rendering of a soldier on a pedestal. He was holding a musket, and I assume he was facing north, although for all *my* dead reckoning and finely tuned sense of direction, he could have been facing south, west, or east. I decided to take my native guide's word for this. After all, we were the people who had wandered in the desert for forty years to cover a trek that should have taken no more than a few weeks, even allowing for the incredible amount of luggage the Israelite women must have packed for the exodus. ("I can't wear this dress again for Sabbath. Miriam and Sarah saw me in this outfit five years ago.") The statue was wearing what appeared to be a Confederate uniform. But concrete was grey anyway, so again I would take Paul at his word but made a mental note in my "What the hell, who's going to know who did it?" file in my brain to paint the uniform

Yankee blue some night and turn it 180 degrees around.

We continued our tour past some neighborhoods of varying prosperity, mostly red brick World War II–era ranch houses interspersed with scattered larger porch-wrapped frame houses of a considerably older vintage. We pulled to a stop in front of a block-long brick structure with a flagpole and bike racks in the center of a long walkway, alongside a sign proclaiming, "Greenville High School, Division A 1975 State Football Champs" in large letters over a list of this year's game schedule.

Paul eased himself out of the car, waved me over to a 6' × 8' granite stone, and proudly proclaimed, "Take a look at this."

I could tell it was some sort of monument to some athletic achievement, but instead it said, "Greenville High School State Mathematics Champion" in a banner over what appeared to be each of the last fifteen years.

"Thought this would surprise your Northern preconceptions. We've got a mediocre team in most sports and do okay in football when we happen to have the talent. But it's come and go, and for the most part, these kids move on in a few years. The math team, on the other hand, is always on top because of their coach, Mr. Cotes, who somehow not only teaches these kids math but also how to excel in it and actually love it. These aren't kids from rich homes but homes without a book in them. A lot have folks that never finished school, and about half are colored. Year after year, he turns them into experts in geometry, calculus, algebra, and trigonometry, the stuff we hated in school. They gladly give up their weekends travelling around the state to tournaments in Mr. Cotes's car or some parent's car, not in school buses like the football team, with the coach paying for the kids whose parents can't.

"Don't get the wrong idea. These kids are by and large well-rounded, not the kids with the taped-together glasses and plastic pocket protectors. Many of them are also on varsity sports teams or leaders in the student government. They're just bright kids with the ability and drive to work hard who just needed someone like Mr. Cotes to show them that math is something that is not mysterious and that they can be good at that too if they try. Most of the time, they come home with the winning trophies, and I would like to say the town appreciates them. But other than this 'math monument' paid for by some anonymous donor"—he winked—"recognition is usually limited to the school newspaper. Colleges, however, are starting to notice these kids, particularly their math SAT scores, and we've had a few go to Harvard and Yale and seem to be really popular with West Point and the Air Force Academy. I guess it's going to take a few years to see where these kids end up, but I suspect many of them will be real leaders that we can be proud to say came from Greenville. Well, enough of the sales pitch. Let's get on home, have a little liquid, and get some dinner."

We headed back up Commerce Street through some of the residential areas and retraced the route I had taken earlier to get to the clinic while Paul pointed out who lived in almost every home, including a little thumbnail bio, as time allowed. While I didn't know anyone he spoke of, it was in a pattern I could not hope to sort out. They had been friends and neighbors for years, and in some cases, generations had played together as children, gone to school together, and often married each other or gone into business together as adults (e.g., "That house over there belonged to Judge So and So, and his daughter married my cousin. And their daughter was my son's English teacher in middle school" or "That's my daddy's house over on the hill, but he moved up the street and built a house next to my brother and rents his old house to my wife's niece and her husband for a fraction of what it's worth just so the family can keep an eye on the drunken SOB").

To make matters more confusing, many family names from previous generations now were used as first names of the next. It was not unusual to have first names like Finley, Braxton, Hamilton, etc. thrown in with an endless assortment of purely Southern nicknames, like Sissy, Boo, Trey, Tut, Buster, and, of course, Bub or Bubba.

With almost every car we passed, Paul would nod his head toward the other driver but more often just raise the index finger of one hand off the steering wheel in an abbreviated wave

"It must be nice to know everyone in town and have them know you too," I commented.

"Well, I do know most everyone, but around here it is assumed that we do know if not like each other, so to not wave or something would be considered rude. In fact, some folks just think they know me but are really waving at the car, and the days when I drive a different car, a whole different set of people wave to me," Paul added.

We drove back toward the interstate and passed the jumble of gas stations and fast-food joints that congregated around interstate exits, to refuel cars and hasten the date with the cardiologist. So far, the neon and plastic intrusion into Greenville was mercifully small, and we were soon surrounded by the Alabama countryside again. We turned off the road and down a long driveway lined with pecan orchards on either side, ending in a circular drive in front of a large—or more correctly, huge—house set on a hill overlooking a small man-made lake. The house was red brick and two-storied, with dormer windows jutting from the roof and a porch draped across its entire front. Not unlike the real-estate ads that describe, "Rocking-chair front porch," this one actually had about a dozen white rockers and assorted end and coffee tables strewn across it.

As we got out of the car, we were greeted enthusiastically by a couple of overly friendly black Labrador retrievers that wagged their bodies from the neck back. They were obviously glad to see Paul, their barking proclaiming, "Daddy's home."

I quickly glanced around for the sound boom and camera crews to confirm that I wasn't actually on a movie set for a rerun of *Gone with the Wind*.

This was nothing like my old neighborhood in Brooklyn except that this one property was probably the same acreage as my entire neighborhood

Centered in the middle of the porch were two massive oak doors, over which hung the largest University of Alabama flag I had ever seen. I was pleased to see that Paul did not bow to the flag nor salute it.

As we entered the main room, I was struck by the massive oak molding and cabinets framing a large walk-in fireplace. I was just taking in the scene when Paul's wife, Anne, entered from the kitchen, smiling and wiping her hands on her apron. She struck me as an attractive lady who carried herself and her age well and seemed to have been taken off the pages of *Southern Living*. She extended her hand and took mine, saying, "David, we're really glad you could join us and hope this will be the first of many visits. From what Paul has already told me, you will always be welcome in our home." She motioned us to a pair of massive leather chairs in front of the fireplace and suggested we have a drink before dinner, reminding Paul that his limit was two drinks before dinner, which would be ready in about twenty minutes.

Paul eagerly made his way to the bar and retrieved two highball glasses filled with Kentucky Bourbon over ice. We sat in front of the fireplace, and he said, "I have a few housekeeping things we need to go over. You may have realized there is not a lot of rental property other than small apartments in Greenville, but we do have several nice houses for sale. I'm sure you can find one that will suit your needs."

At this point, I reminded Paul of my newly divorced finances and that I did not have anything like the money to purchase a house. I mentioned to him that I also was committed to a lease on a rental apartment in Montgomery that had about seven more months to run.

He told me not to worry about that; they would buy out my lease, and he had already spoken to the bank president, who offered to loan me 150 percent of the cost of any house I wanted, which would be an interest-only loan until I'd settled in and began enjoying some positive cash flow.

I asked him how that was possible, and he winked and went on to add that his family foundation owned the bank, and they were prepared to take care of me if I came on board.

Speaking of money, as far as salary was concerned, I could start at twice the level that was being paid in Montgomery, and then if everything went well, I would become a full partner the following year.

He also mentioned that part of my job would be to get to know the people at the country club, hang out there, and make friends. I guessed from the expression on my face that he knew that I had some misgivings about that, but he assured me that they did not restrict membership based on race or religion and that I would be welcome. He added, "Just wait till the drug reps find out that you are from the Nawth, and they fall all over themselves to teach you about our Southern ways."

As near as I figured, these fine folks had just made me an offer I couldn't refuse.

As if on cue, Anne emerged the kitchen and said, "You boys can come in for dinner now after you wash up."

We did as we were told, and Anne led us into the largest dining room I had ever seen. I could just picture my father conducting a Passover Seder with all my relatives around *that* table. Paul asked me if I wanted to say grace, and fortunately, I had anticipated this (or maybe it was my alleged training in parapsychology). I managed to recall one Hebrew prayer and hoped I would not mess up the lines.

At this point, Anne and a few cooks emerged from the kitchen with plates of fried okra, hush puppies, mashed potatoes and gravy, biscuits, and the biggest mound of fried chicken I had ever seen. It was obvious that this sort of meal had a lot to do with Paul's habitus, and if I continued to eat like this, we would soon look like twins.

During dinner Anne explained that her people were from the Mobile area, where she, too, came from a rather large family that had lived there for several generations and were involved in the shipping business. She and Paul met when they were students at the University of Alabama and rather quickly decided to marry and return to the Greenville area. They had three children who were all away at school, one of whom was already thinking about medical school. It was anticipated that they would find suitable mates at the university and hopefully with knowledge that it must be someone who would fit in with the family. They said that just when your kids were no longer teenagers and you could love them again, they'd come home with someone you couldn't stand. They were hoping this would not be the case.

Over coffee and pecan pie with ice cream for dessert, Anne leaned close to me and took my hand. "David, the whole family that you've met today has a really good opinion of you, but I want to add one thing. I know that you were recently divorced, and your world was turned upside down. My younger brother got divorced at about your age and struggled to maintain his relationship with his kids. I want you to know that to some extent, we know what you're going through, and we will do everything to make the transition into joining the Strickler family go as smoothly as possible. I hope you won't consider this just another job, but by coming to Greenville, we would like you to feel that you are coming home again to a place you've never been before. Welcome to your new family."

The end and the *new beginning*

About the Author

avid Guttman was born and raised in Brooklyn, New York, and lived there for seventeen years. And he hated every minute of it. He attended Madison high school, the same school Ruth Bader Ginsburg, senator Bernie Sanders, and senator Chuck Schumer attended. Because of a difference in their ages, David has never met any of them but knows they would've been good friends.

After high school, he went to St. Lawrence University for a bachelor's degree in chemistry, followed by a master's degree from Cornell University and a PhD from Tulane University. He spent four years in Colombia, doing research in entomology, and then attended Creighton University, where he got an MD followed by a residency in pediatrics at Albany Medical Center.

From the time David started college until he finished his residency, he spent seventeen years, and his father used to joke that he was the oldest living premed in the country. David became a board-certified pediatrician and practiced pediatrics for more than forty years. He knows he took the long way around, but he wouldn't change it for anything. David has retired from medicine and now devotes his time to writing. He thanks his mother for teaching him to read when the school said he was hopeless.

www.ingramcontent.com/pod-product-compliance
Lightning Source LLC
Chambersburg PA
CBHW020326180726
47991CB00019B/885